THE COMPLETE PIANO PLAYER
STYLE BOOK

'By the end of this book you will
be putting all your piano-playing skills
to work in a number of fascinating new styles.
You will be playing 22 popular songs,
including: *Bridge Over Troubled Water,
Ballade Pour Adeline, Money, Money, Money,*
and *The James Bond Theme*.'

Kenneth Baker

HAL•LEONARD®

Exclusive distributors:

Hal Leonard
7777 West Bluemound Road, Milwaukee, WI 53213
Email: info@halleonard.com
Hal Leonard Europe Limited
42 Wigmore Street Maryleborne, London, WIU 2 RN
Email: info@halleonardeurope.com
Hal Leonard Australia Pty. Ltd.
4 Lentara Court Cheltenham, Victoria, 9132 Australia
Email: info@halleonard.com.au

ISBN 0.7119.0461.8
Order No. AM35338
This book © Copyright 1984 by Hal Leonard

Designed by Howard Brown
Photography by Peter Wood
Arranged by Kenneth Baker

Printed in EU.

www.halleonard.com

CONTENTS

ABOUT THIS BOOK

This is the last book in 'The Complete Piano Player' series.

To help you become a complete, all-round player, it has been arranged as a series of piano **styles**. You will learn Boogie Style, Block Chord Style, Country Style, Modern Blues Style, Unison Octave Style, and so on.

As usual, you will be working with popular standards and famous hit songs, interspersed with a few tuneful classics.

You need not play every piece in the exact order given. For example, although the three Boogie Woogie pieces are placed together for convenience, you could insert a slower number, such as 'Stardust', or one of the two Minuets in between, as light relief.

Don't lose touch with Books One to Five of the series. Most of your basic information is there, and will need revising from time to time.

To build your repertoire further, look at 'The Complete Piano Player Songbooks'. These are available at various levels of difficulty.

Good luck with your piano playing.

NEW NOTES:
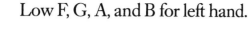

1   Low F, G, A, and B for left hand.

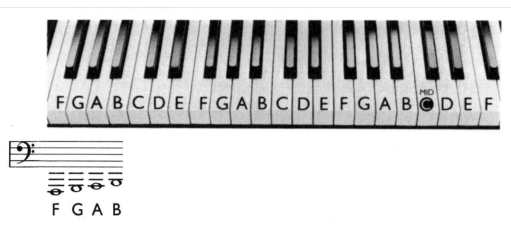

FOUR IN A BAR AND EIGHT IN A BAR POP STYLE

2   In this simple but effective style your left hand plays a chord, or octave, on every beat of the bar:

For variation your left hand can play twice as many chords – one chord on each quaver of the bar:

Although the left hand seems simple enough, this style usually involves a good deal of syncopation in the right hand. As with all syncopated pieces, keep your left hand rock-steady throughout.

CECILIA

Words & Music: Paul Simon

Cel - ia, You're break-ing my heart___ You're shak-ing my con - fi - dence

(no pedal)

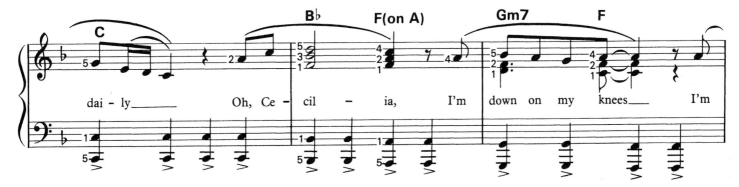

dai - ly_____ Oh, Ce - cil - ia, I'm down on my knees___ I'm

beg-ging you please to come home___ Ho ho home___ Ma-king love___ in the

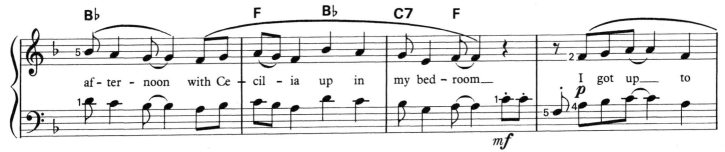

af - ter - noon with Ce - cil - ia up in my bed - room___ I got up___ to

wash my face___ when I come back to bed___ some-one's tak - en my place.___

MONEY, MONEY, MONEY

Words & Music: Benny Andersson & Bjorn Ulvaeus

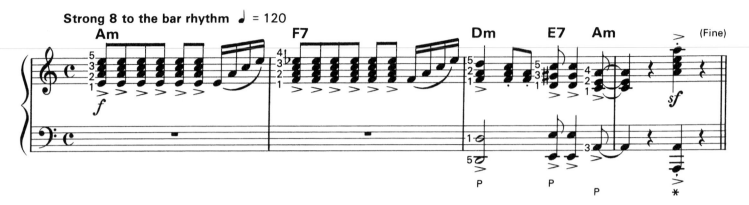

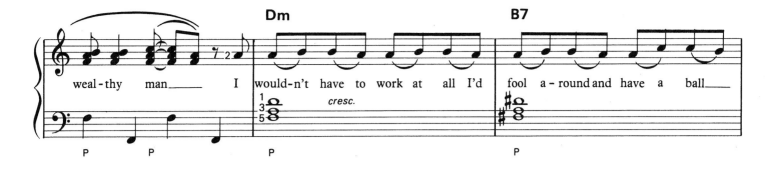

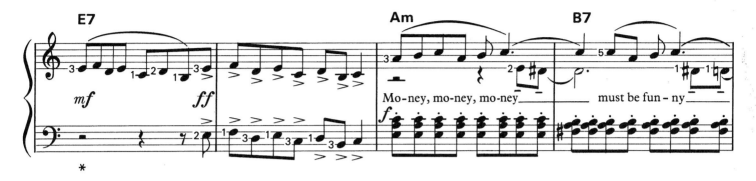

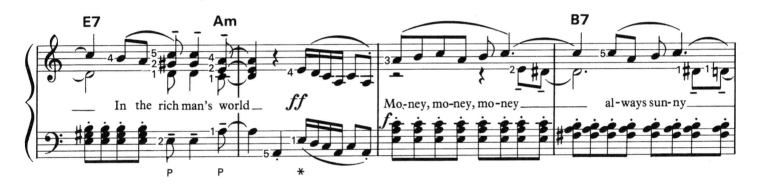

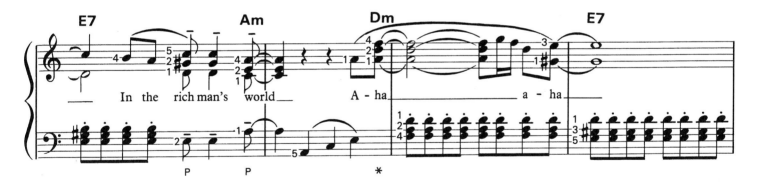

BRUBECK STYLE

3

The Dave Brubeck Quartet was well known in the '50s for its own particular brand of Modern Jazz.

The following piece, *Take Five*, was written by the group's alto saxophonist: Paul Desmond. The Time Signature is unusual: five crotchets (quarter notes) in a bar. Think of these as **three** crotchets followed by **two**. The basic left hand figure, which appears in Bar 1, will give you the feel of the rhythm.

TAKE FIVE
By Paul Desmond

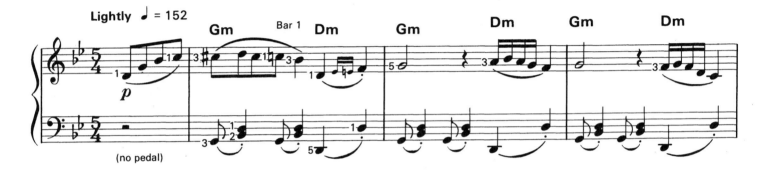

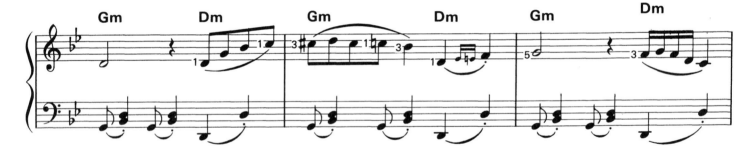

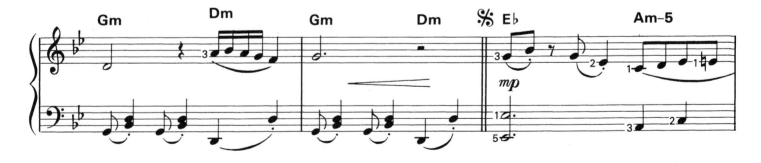

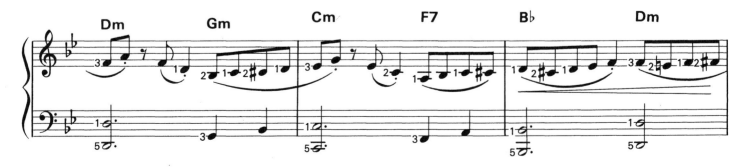

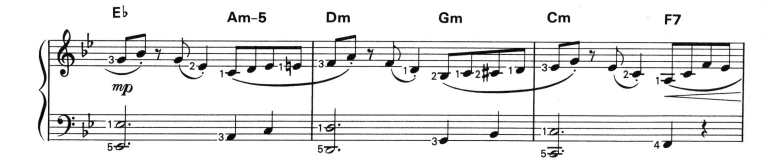

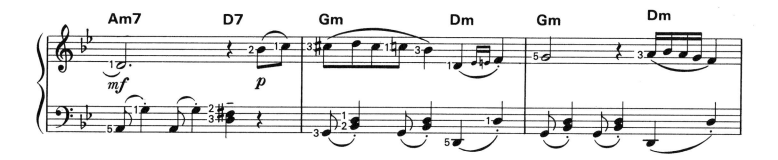

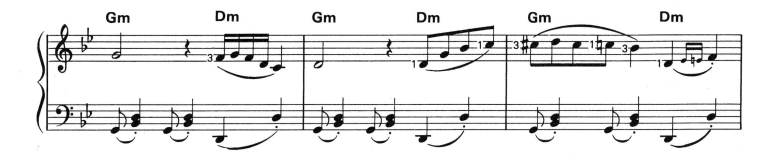

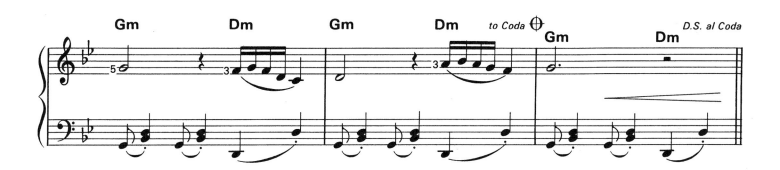

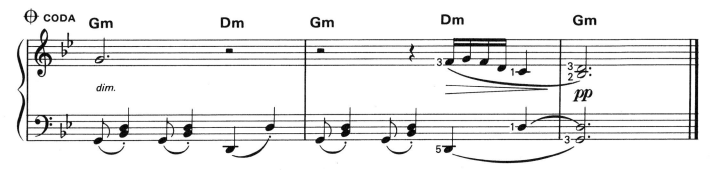

OFF BEAT STYLE

4

Playing on the 'off beat' means playing in between the main beats of a piece. In Hoagy Carmichael's famous *Stardust,* you generate a nice rhythmic flow by playing 'off beat' chords softly with your right hand while your left hand plays melody notes on the beat (see Bars 1 and 2, for example).

In Bars 11 and 12 the situation is reversed: your left hand plays off beat 'G's' while your right hand plays the melody (on the beat).

STARDUST
Words: Mitchell Parish. Music: Hoagy Carmichael

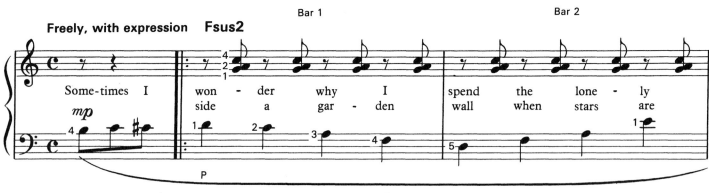

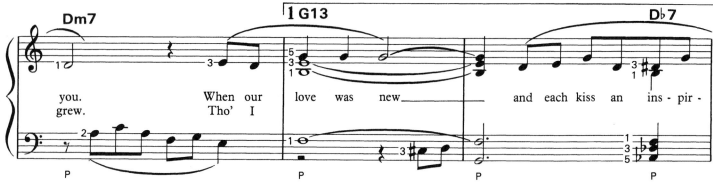

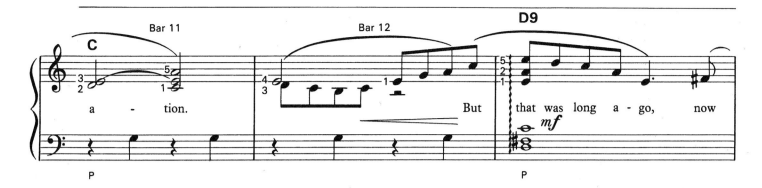

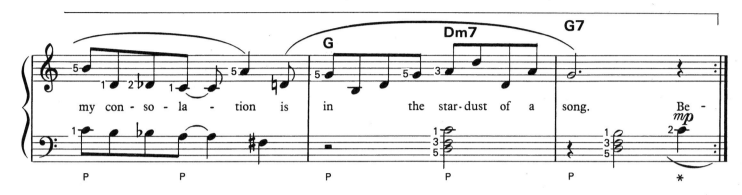

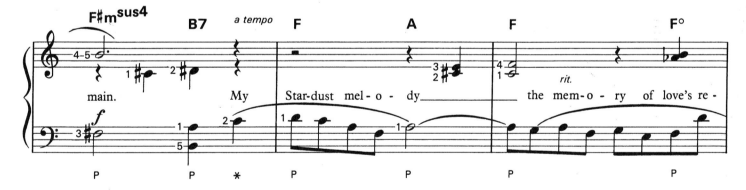

***Broadening**–decreasing the speed.

BOOGIE WOOGIE STYLE

5

Boogie Woogie is a piano style which developed out of the 'Blues'. Based on the same harmonies as the Blues, Boogie Woogie tends to be more lively and outgoing. Its most characteristic feature is its repeating bass patterns. In the three Boogie-style pieces which follow you will have a chance to practise three typical left hand Boogie patterns:

1. GET BACK (p. 15)

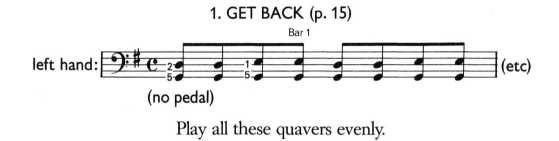

Play all these quavers evenly.

2. NIGHT TRAIN (p. 16)

Here the quavers are NOT even.
Play these left hand figures with a 'lilt', like this:

NIGHT TRAIN

3. BLUE SUEDE SHOES (p. 18)

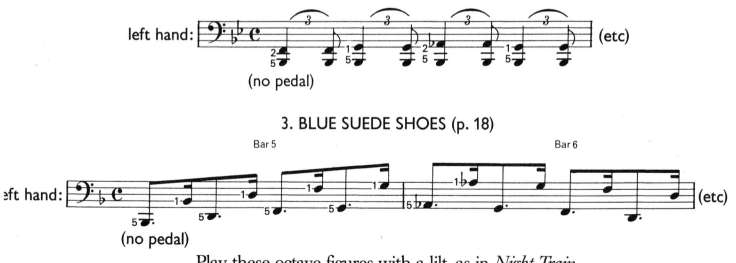

Play these octave figures with a lilt, as in *Night Train*.

Remember: When playing Boogie Woogie your touch must be firm and your rhythm rock-steady.

GET BACK

Words & Music: John Lennon & Paul McCartney

Medium Boogie ♩ =126

mf Jo Jo was a man who thought he was a lon-er, but he knew it could-n't last

Jo Jo left his home in Tuc-son, Ar-i-zo-na, for

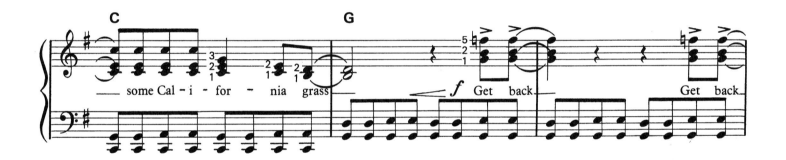

some Cal-i-for-nia grass f Get back. Get back

Get back to where you once be-longed Get back

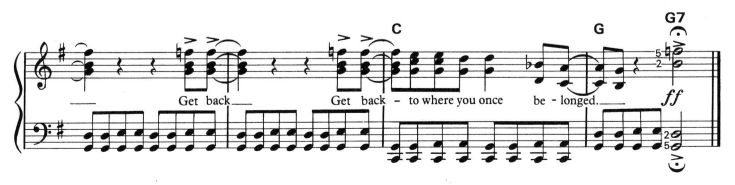

Get back Get back to where you once be-longed. ff

THE TREMOLO AGAIN

6

In Bar 2 of *Night Train* (and elsewhere in the same piece), you will see an alternative way of writing a 'tremolo':

Turn back to page 42 in Book Five of *The Complete Piano Player* and read again about how to do 'tremolos'.

NIGHT TRAIN

Words: Oscar Washington and Lewis C. Simpkins. Music: Jimmy Forrest.

mo-ther said I'd lose her if I ev - er did a-buse her, should have list - ened.

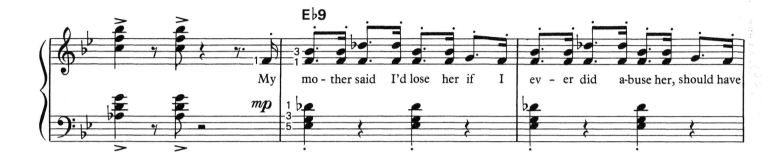

My mo - ther said I'd lose her if I ev - er did a-buse her, should have

list - ened. Now I have learned my less - on, my sweet

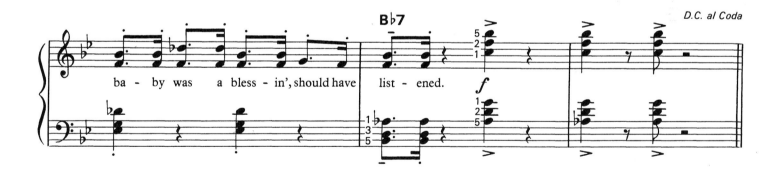

ba - by was a bless - in', should have list - ened.

D.C. al Coda

CODA

blues she left just won't set me free.

ROCK 'N' ROLL STYLE

7

Blue Suede Shoes, recorded by Elvis Presley in 1956, is one of the most famous rock 'n' roll songs.

This arrangement uses the most active of our three Boogie Woogie bass patterns. When practising it, stress the left hand fifth finger notes.

BLUE SUEDE SHOES

Words & Music: Carl Lee Perkins

Well it's one for the mo – ney, two for the show, three to get read – y now

go, cat, go, but don't you step on my Blue___ Suede

Shoes. You can do an–y–thing, but lay

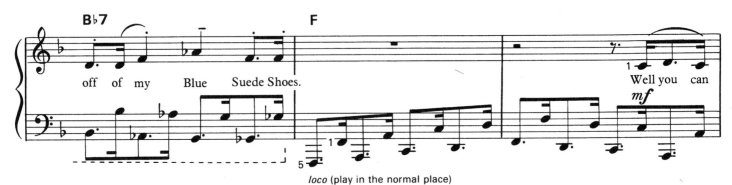

off of my Blue Suede Shoes. Well you can

loco (play in the normal place)

* Play one octave (eight notes) lower than written.

18

knock me down. Step in my face. Slan-der my name all o – ver the place

Do an – y thing that you want – to do. But uh___ uh, – ho – ney, lay

off of my shoes. Don't you step on my Blue__ Suede__

Shoes. You can do an – y – thing but lay

off of my Blue Suede Shoes.

MINUET STYLE

8

The Minuet, a graceful dance of French origin, was popular in the 17th and 18th Centuries. It is in ¾ Time.

Here are two famous Minuets, one written specially for the piano by Beethoven, the other taken from a string quartet by Boccherini.

MINUET IN G
By: Ludwig Van Beethoven

MINUET (FROM "STRING QUARTET")

By Luigi Boccherini

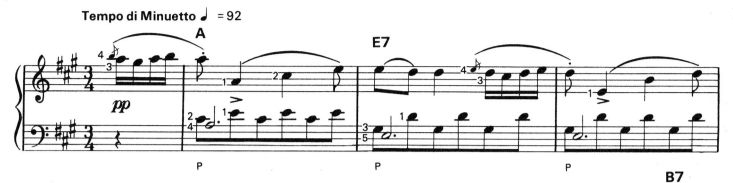

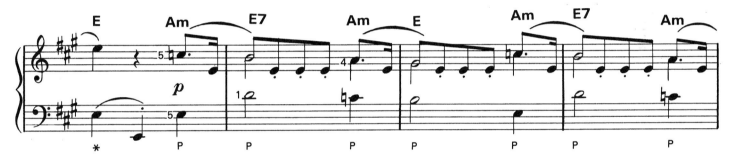

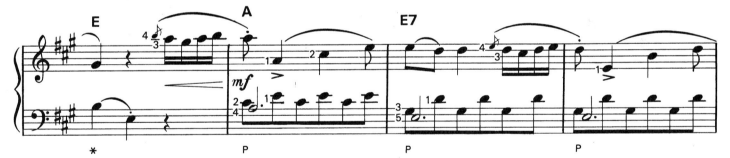

*Trill, or shake. An ornament consisting
of the rapid alternation of the written
note and the note directly above it.
For the first trill (above) use F♯ and G♯,
for the second trill (above) use B and C♯.

MODERN BLUES STYLE

9

Many of the original Blues songs and instrumental solos were based on a simple 12-bar harmonic sequence. You have already played two pieces of this type: *Swingin' Shepherd Blues* (Book Five, page 14), and *Night Train* (Book Six, page 16).

The next piece, *Like Young*, by André Previn, is a blues written in a Modern Jazz style. In addition to the usual twelve bars based on blues harmonies, there are eight extra bars inserted into the middle for contrast. These 'middle 8' bars modulate skilfully through the keys of G, A flat, and A, before returning to the original key of B flat for a repeat of the main theme.

LIKE YOUNG

By: André Previn

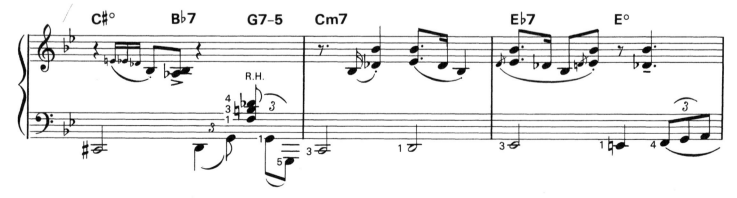

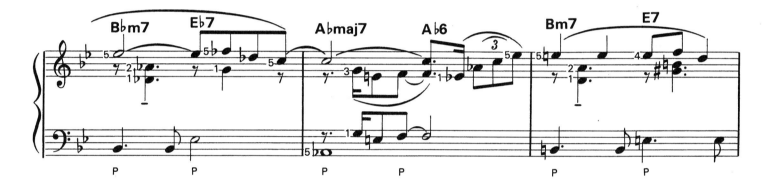

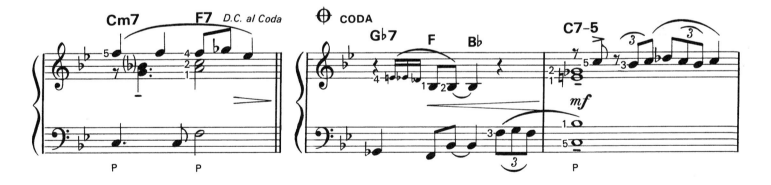

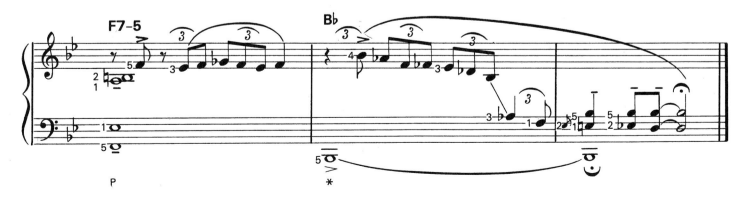

MOVING SEMITONE CHORD STYLE

10

A semitone, or half step, is the distance between any piano key and the next nearest key (black or white):

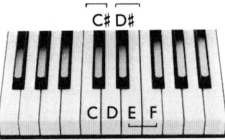

examples of semitones

In the next piece: *One Note Samba,* you play a full chord style in which the chords move almost continuously in semitones. This semitone movement is usually downwards (Bars 1-15, for example), but is occasionally upwards (Bars 19, 20, 23).

Study each hand separately and note carefully where the semitone movements occur.

ONE NOTE SAMBA (SAMBA DE UMA NOTA SO)

Music: Antonio Carlos Jobim. Original Words: N. Mendonca. English Lyric: Jon Hendricks

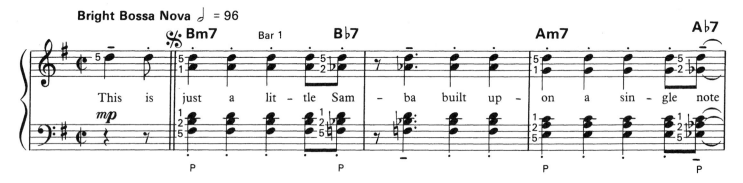

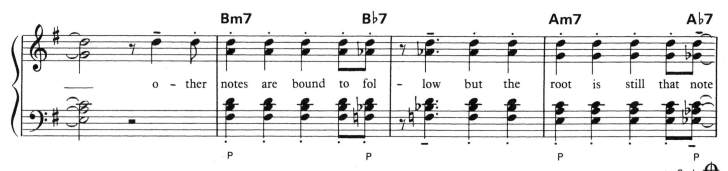

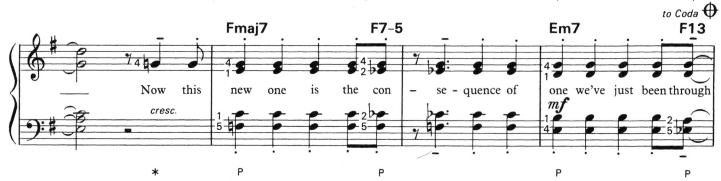

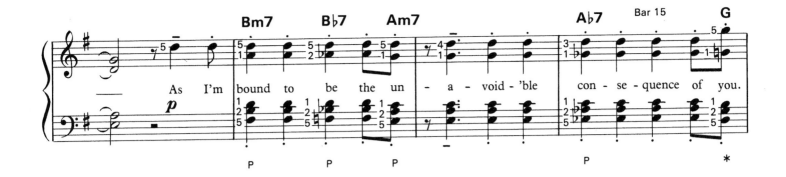

As I'm bound to be the un-a-void-'ble con-se-quence of you.

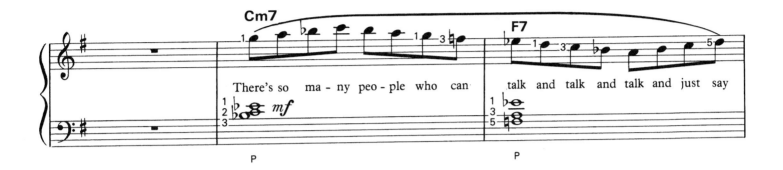

There's so ma-ny peo-ple who can talk and talk and talk and just say

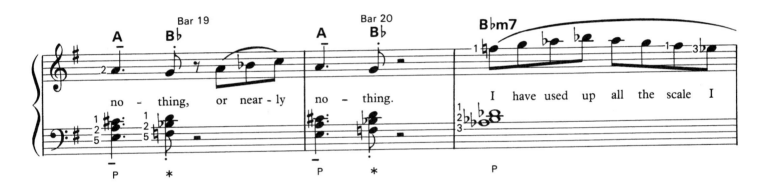

no-thing, or near-ly no-thing. I have used up all the scale I

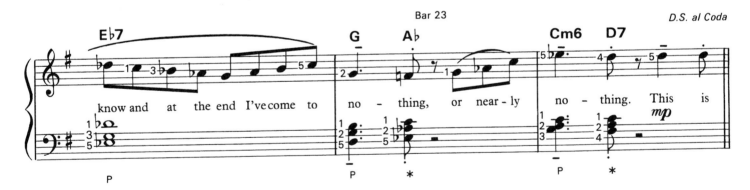

know and at the end I've come to no-thing, or near-ly no-thing. This is

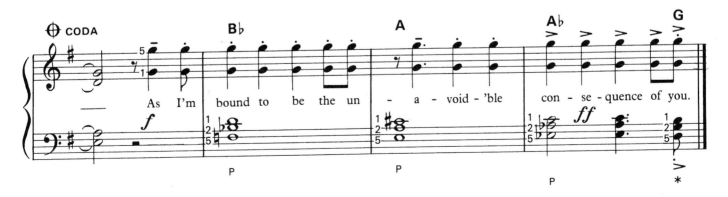

As I'm bound to be the un-a-void-'ble con-se-quence of you.

PERCUSSIVE STYLE

The *James Bond Theme* relies for its effect on a hard, percussive style of playing.

The piece starts dramatically with a legato left hand counter melody which has become famous. As well as playing this counter melody, your left hand plays repeated bass E's, staccato, to keep the rhythm going. Above this your right hand plays off beat chords (see Off-Beat Style, page 12).

The main theme begins at Bar 5, with spiky, repeated chords in the right hand.

The Middle Section of the piece (marked 'swingy'), is driven along by a solid 4-to-a-bar left hand, moving mainly in semitones.

In the **Coda** both hands play the same notes, so simply copy your right hand with your left. Observe the phrasing here. The piece ends with a discordant two-handed tremolo, played very loudly.

THE JAMES BOND THEME

By John Barry

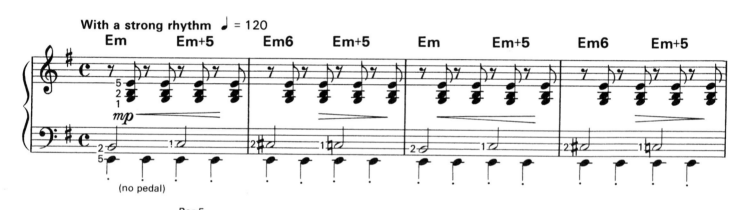

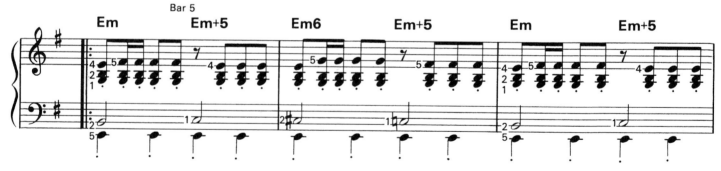

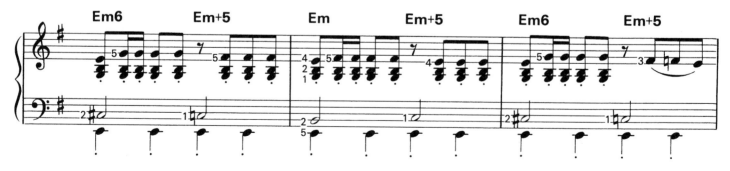

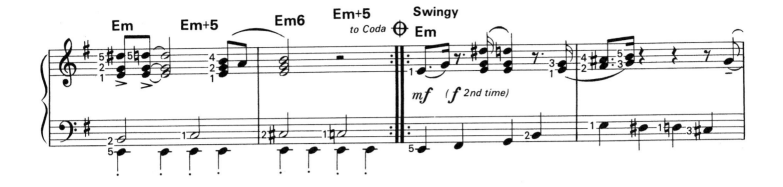

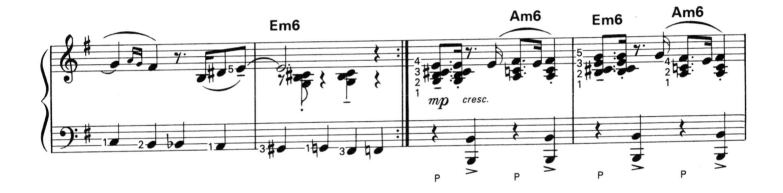

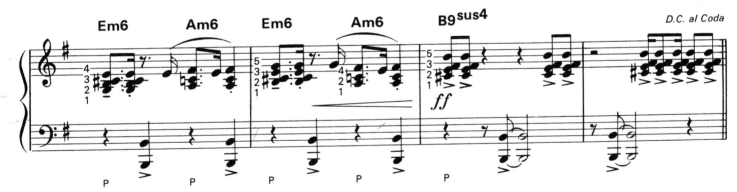

RICHARD CLAYDERMAN STYLE

12

Richard Clayderman is a young pianist who brings a classical piano style to popular music.

For much of *Ballade Pour Adeline* your left hand plays an 'open broken chord' type of accompaniment (see Book Five, page 46).

Notice the solitary $\frac{2}{4}$ Bar (Bar 14) in amongst the $\frac{4}{4}$ bars. Think of this as an incomplete bar. Count 1, 2, then carry on again from '1', as if nothing had happened.

A 'wrist staccato' technique (see Book Two, page 44) is called for in the right hand in Bars 2, 5, 6, and elsewhere.

BALLADE POUR ADELINE

Composer: Paul de Senneville

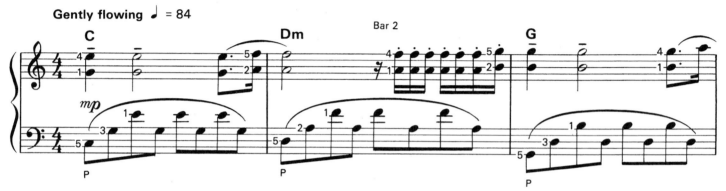

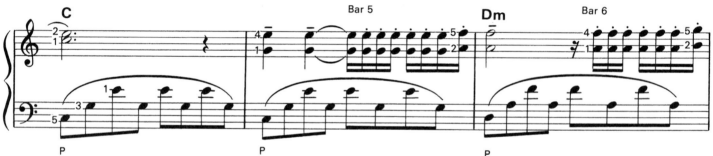

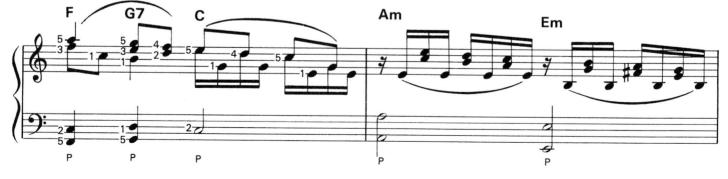

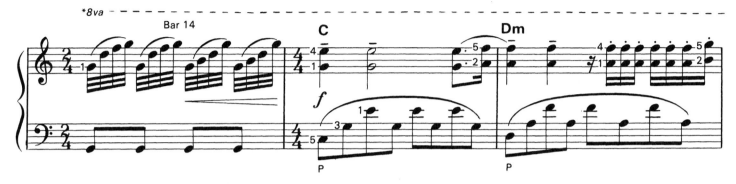

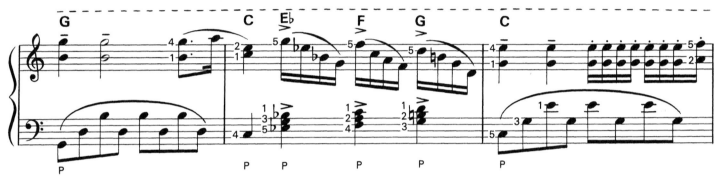

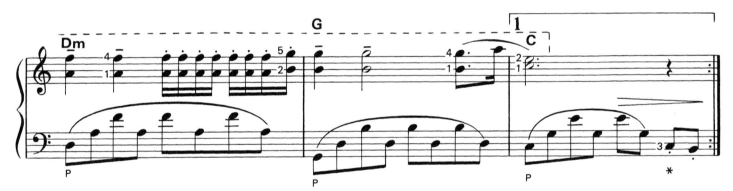

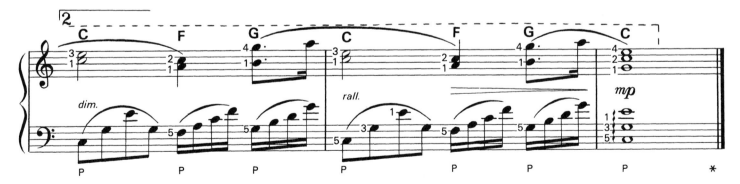

*Play one octave (eight notes) higher
than written.

COUNTRY STYLE

13 This is an American popular music style, notable for its simple harmonies and uncomplicated rhythms.

Originally country music was played on fretted stringed instruments such as guitar, banjo, and mandolin. Country style piano playing tends to imitate these instruments in some respects. One of the most common characteristics of the style is the 'hammer on' technique, common in guitar playing. Here the guitarist plucks an open string, then quickly places his finger on the same string, causing the note to rise (usually to the next highest note):

IT'S ALL IN THE GAME (Bar 2)

with an upper note added:

hammering on

Another device borrowed from fretted instrument players is 'finger-picking'. This is where the guitarist (or banjoist) alternates in his right hand between the thumb and other fingers. You will find examples of this technique adapted to the piano in Bars 8 and 13 (right hand).

IT'S ALL IN THE GAME
Music: Charles G. Dawes. Words: Carl Sigman

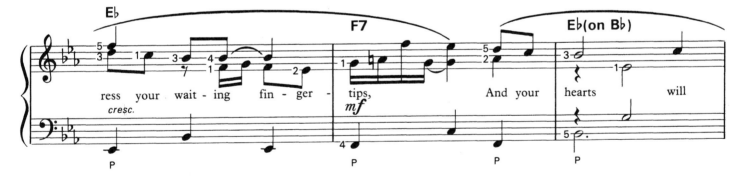

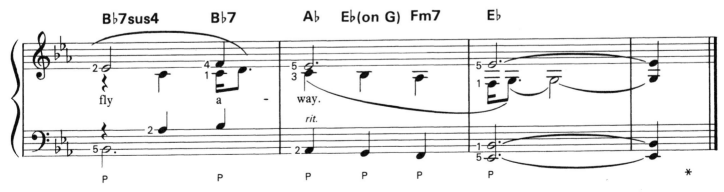

BLOCK CHORD STYLE

14

This style was developed for the piano by George Shearing in the late '40s.

The two main elements of the style are:
1. The right hand plays the melody in chords.
2. The left hand doubles the melody, in single notes only, one octave lower.

In Bars 9–18 of *Don't Blame Me*, I have changed from block chord style to open chord style for the sake of contrast.

DON'T BLAME ME

Words & Music: Jimmy McHugh and Dorothy Fields

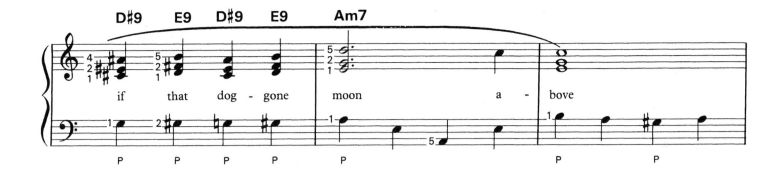

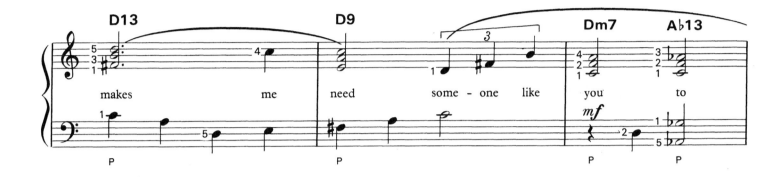

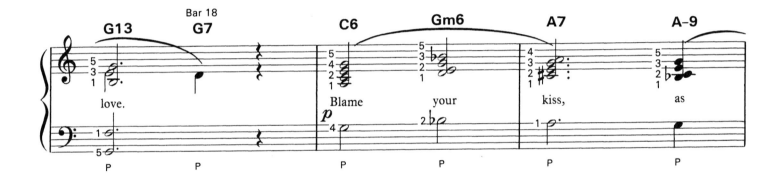

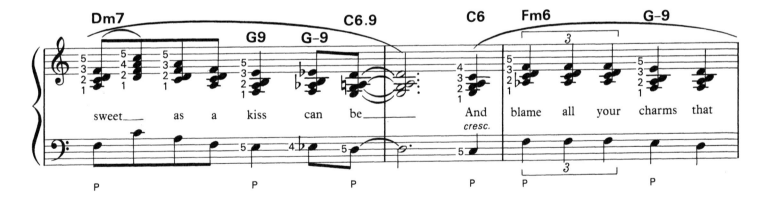

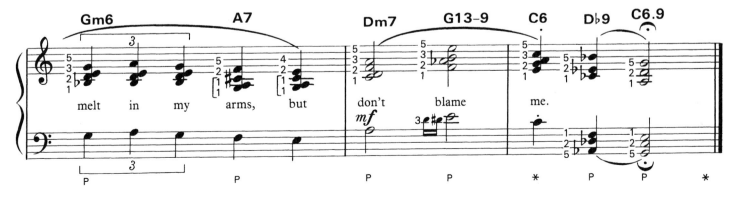

Lullaby of Birdland is George Shearing's own composition.

The Middle Section (Bars 11–18) is written in Block Chord style. To make this part easier to play, quite a few single notes have been used in the right hand. This is common practice when playing block chords in faster pieces.

LULLABY OF BIRDLAND

Music: George Shearing. Words George David Weiss

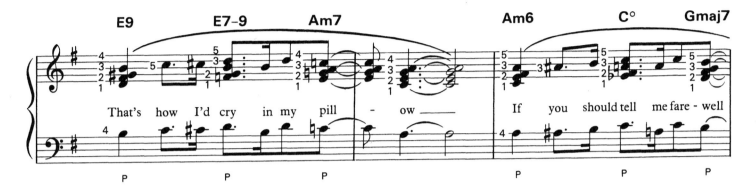

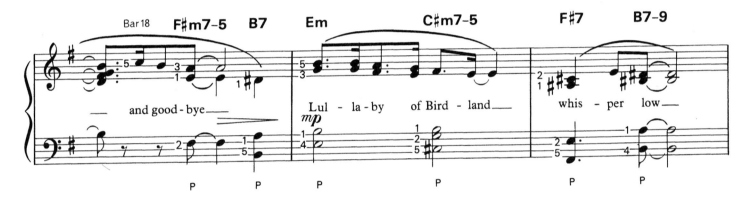

UNISON OCTAVE STYLE

15

This is a brilliant and impressive solo style for piano, but it does involve a lot of jumping about.

The melody is played by both hands in unison, two octaves apart. In between playing melody notes both hands travel down the keyboard to add accompanying chords.

As with *Gymnopédie No 1*, in Book Five (page 22), you must get used to finding your place in the music after looking down at the keyboard.

MARIA ELENA

Music: Lorenzo Barcelata. English lyric: S.K. Russell

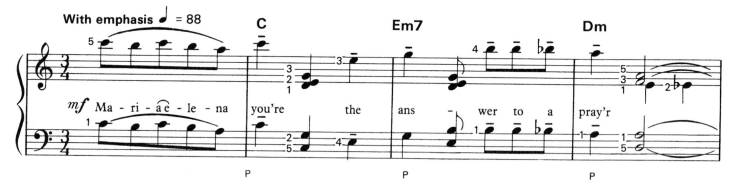

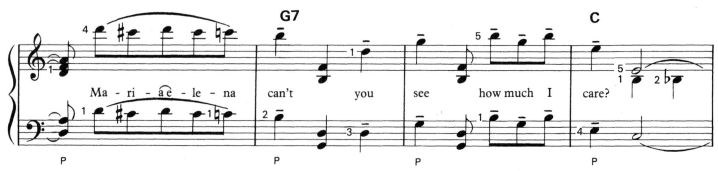

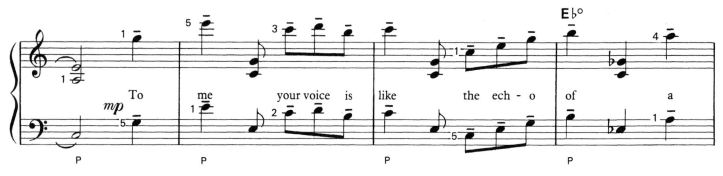

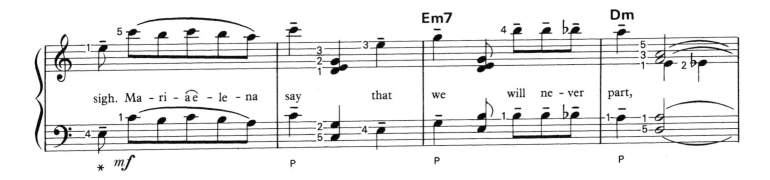

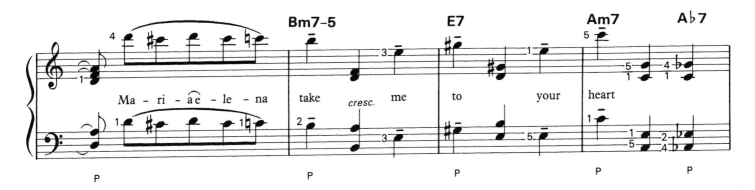

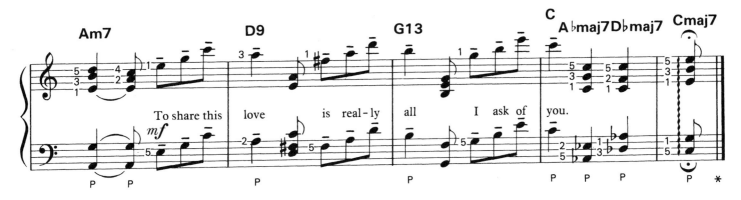

FAST LATIN STYLE

16 In *Mrs Robinson* your left hand plays the basic Bossa Nova rhythm pattern given in Book Four, page 44:

but with variations:

MRS ROBINSON

MRS ROBINSON

Words & Music: Paul Simon

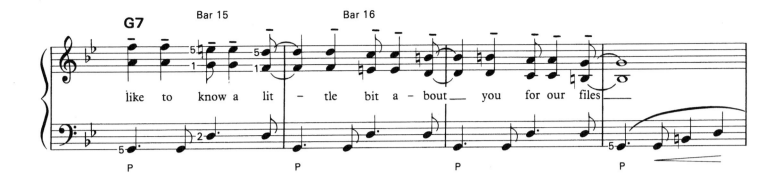

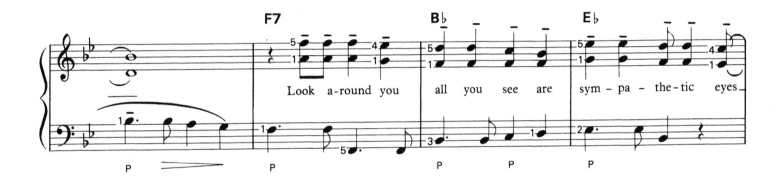

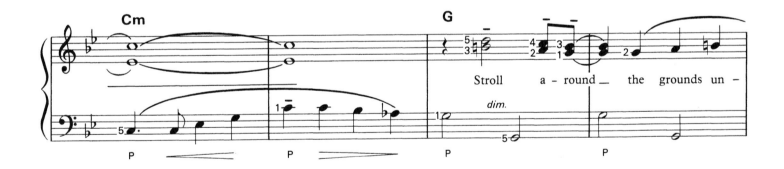

NOVELTY PIANO STYLE

17 Novelty piano solos were popular in the '20s, and beyond. They were usually based on 'swing' piano styles, the basic accompaniments of which consisted of:

'bass note, chord, bass note, chord', and so on.

One of the best of these novelty pieces is *Nola*:

NOLA

By: Felix Arndt

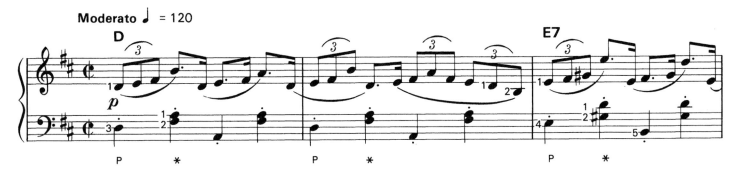

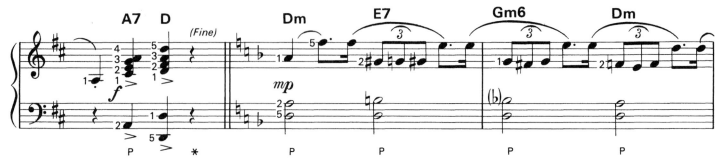

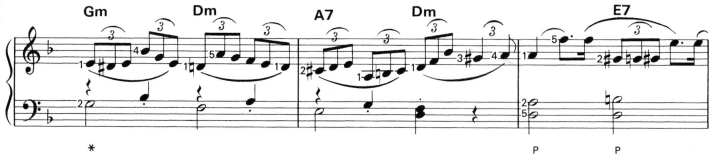

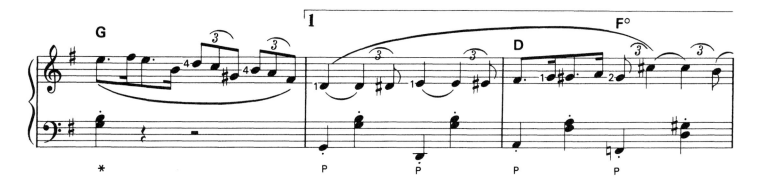

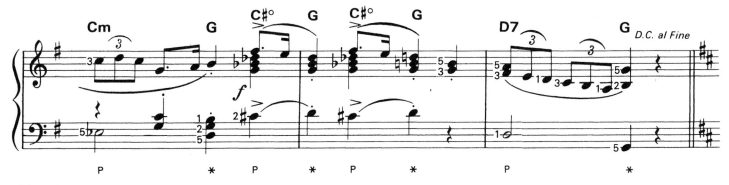

CONTEMPORARY FOLK STYLE

18 In this style modern musical techniques (such as new rhythms, the use of amplified instruments, etc), are applied to traditional style songs.

In *Bridge Over Troubled Water,* a huge success for Simon and Garfunkel in 1970, a Bossa Nova bass line has been added to the song in order to give it a modern style rhythm.

BRIDGE OVER TROUBLED WATER

Words & Music: Paul Simon

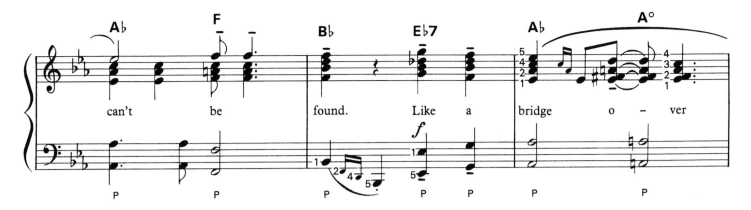

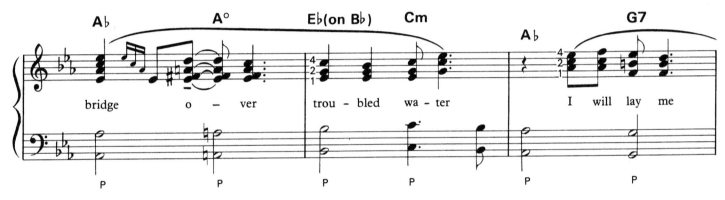

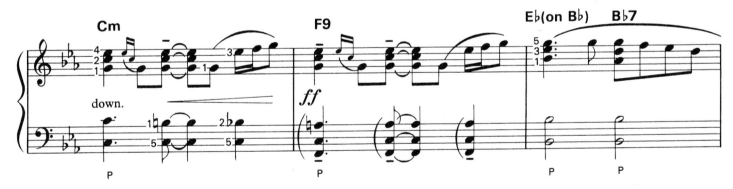

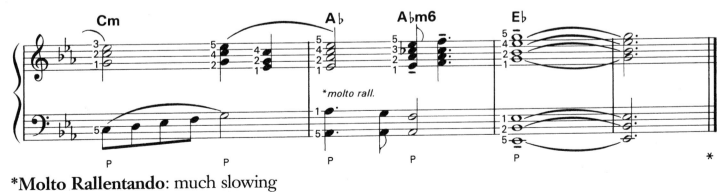

*Molto Rallentando: *much slowing* down

ROCK BOOGIE STYLE

19 This is a mixture of a modern rock style tune with a boogie woogie bass line.

In *Lady Madonna*, one of The Beatles' later recordings, there is a fine, varied 8 to the bar bass line, which combines boogie patterns with a walking bass. The climax of the piece comes in Bars 15 and 16, where the bass movement stops, temporarily. The theme and boogie bass then pick up again and we go out comparatively quietly.

LADY MADONNA

Words & Music: John Lennon and Paul McCartney

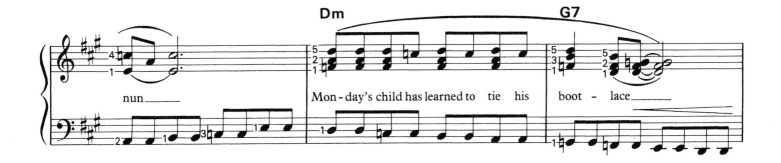

nun___ Mon-day's child has learned to tie his boot-lace___

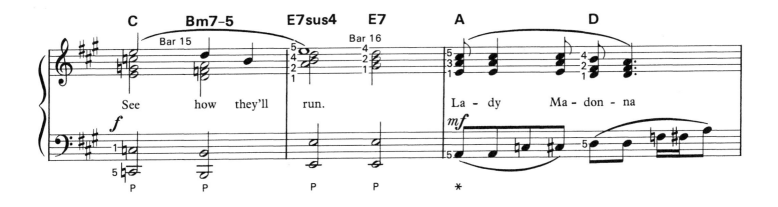

See how they'll run. La-dy Ma-don-na

Ba-by at your breast Won-der how you man-aged to feed___ the rest___

La-dy Ma-don-na ly-ing on the bed lis-ten to the mu-sic play-ing

in your head.___

LAST WORD

This is the end of The Complete Piano Player Style Book, the last book in The Complete Piano Player series. You can now consider yourself a good, all-round pianist. But you do need to enlarge your repertoire. For this, use The Complete Piano Player Songbooks. They contain fabulous new pieces at all levels, written in the style of The Complete Piano Player books.

We end this book on piano styles with a classical piece by one of the greatest stylists in music: Edvard Grieg.

WEDDING DAY AT TROLDHAUGEN

By: Edvard Grieg

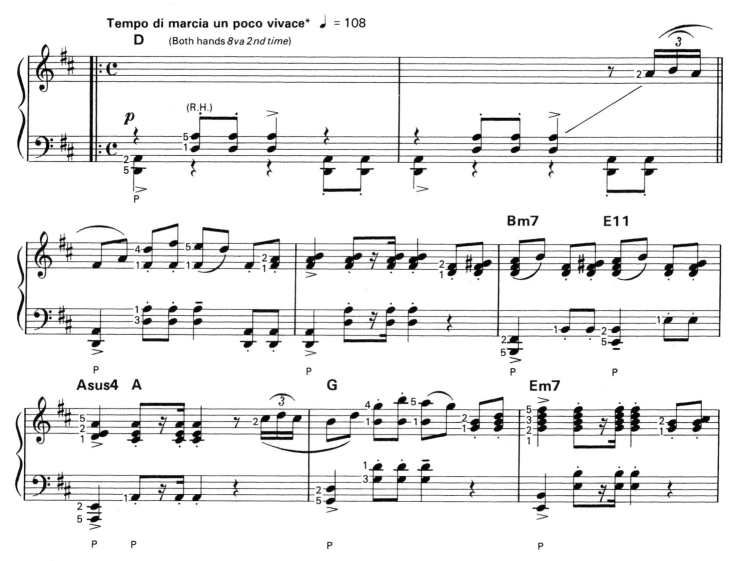

*March tempo, but a little more lively

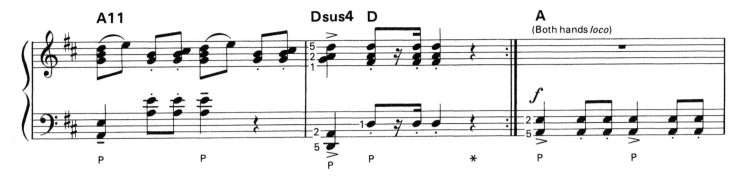

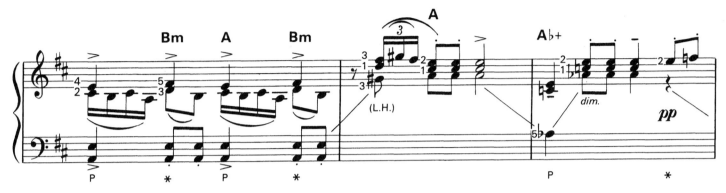

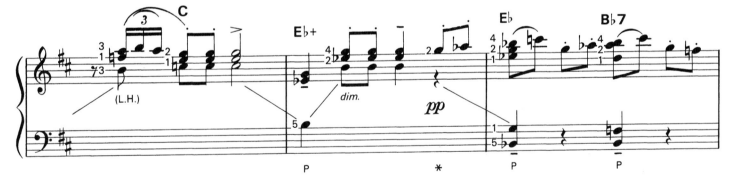

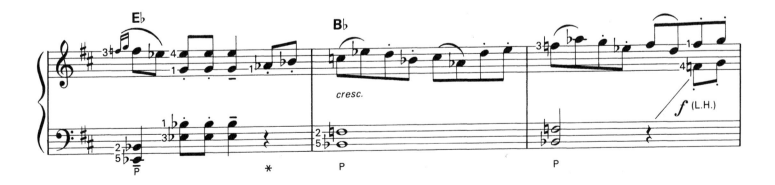

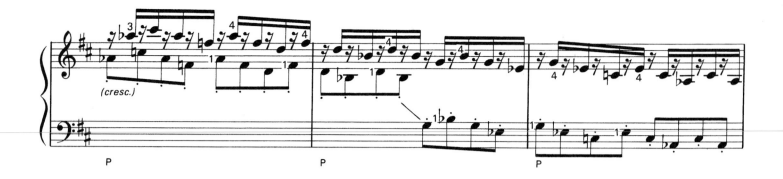

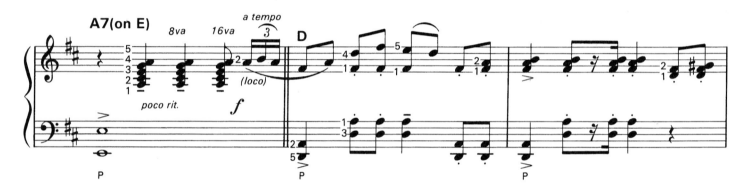

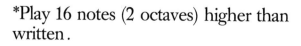

*Play 16 notes (2 octaves) higher than written.